.11/13

J179.7
COST

1035279

D0854821

LaRue
201 S. Lincoln Blvd
Hodgenville, KY 42748
(270) 358-3851

Both Sides of the Story
EUTHANASIA

EUTHANASIA

Patience Coster

rosen publishing's
rosen central

NEW YORK

This edition first published in 2013 by:

The Rosen Publishing Group, Inc.
29 East 21st Street, New York, NY 10010

Copyright © 2013 Arcturus Publishing Limited

First Edition

All rights reserved. No part of this book may be reproduced in any form without permission in writing from the publisher, except by a reviewer.

Editors: Nicola Barber and Joe Harris
U.S. Editor: Kathy Campbell
Picture researcher: Nicola Barber
Designer: Ian Winton

Picture credits: Corbis: cover right and 20 (Mark Costantini/San Francisco Chronicle), title page and 35 (Jason Reed/Reuters), 22 (Colin McPherson), 25 (Bettmann), 29 (Tom Fox/Dallas Morning News), 30 (Richard Clement/Reuters), 33 (Steffen Schmidt/epa), 38 (Jeff Kowalsky/ZUMA Press), 41 (John Van Hasselt). Science Photo Library: 17 (Southern Illinois University). Shutterstock: cover left (Wallenrock), 7 (federicofoto), 9 (Creatista), 11 (Zoltan Pataki), 12 (William Casey), 14 (Ingvald Kaldhussater), 19 (David Castillo Dominici), 27 (M. Bonotto), 37 (Dennis Sabo), 42 (beerkoff).

Library of Congress Cataloging-in-Publication Data

Coster, Patience.
 Euthanasia / Patience Coster. -- First edition.
    pages cm. -- (Both sides of the story)
 Includes bibliographical references and index.
 ISBN 978-1-4488-7186-5 (library binding : alk. paper)
 1. Euthanasia--Juvenile literature. I. Title.
 R726.C6768 2013
 179.7--dc23
                        2012026948

Manufactured in China

CPSIA Compliance Information: Batch #W13YA: For further information, contact Rosen Publishing, New York, New York, at 1-800-237-9932.

Contents

A Matter of Life and Death

Is it ever acceptable to help another person to die? Or is the taking of human life simply wrong? Euthanasia—the intentional ending of a life in order to relieve pain and suffering—raises many ethical questions. Although forbidden by law in most countries in the world, euthanasia has a growing number of supporters who believe it should be legalized.

A universal truth

Death is one of the few certainties in life—it is something we must all face. Despite this universal truth, most people don't like talking about death. Perhaps they find it depressing or frightening, or maybe they simply don't see the point in discussing the inevitable, believing that "what will be, will be." In spite of this unwillingness, the arguments raging around the legalization of euthanasia force us to think about death and the ethical issues surrounding it.

Good death?

The word euthanasia derives from the Greek meaning "happy or fortunate in death" (or "good death"). The origins of the term therefore emphasize the positive—the concept of free will and the right to choose, based on the human ability to reason. Supporters of euthanasia argue that people with terminal or degenerative illnesses (illnesses in which the body's system gradually breaks down) should be allowed to choose death over suffering. They believe this is the mark of a civilized and compassionate society. They say that other people should be allowed to help an individual to die, if this is what that person wants.

The right to choose?

"Whose body is this?"

Sue Rodriguez, who was diagnosed with a degenerative disease and, in 1993, was refused the right to die by the Supreme Court in Canada

Tombstones in a graveyard remind us that death is a certainty. Supporters of euthanasia argue that a "good death" is both desirable and possible.

The right to die?

"When people ask me about the 'right to die,' I respond, 'Don't worry—you won't miss out on it!'"

Father Frank Pavone, Priests for Life

Opponents believe the practice of euthanasia is dangerous and open to abuse. They argue that it undermines respect for the sanctity of life (the view that all human life is sacred) and gives too much power to doctors and other health professionals. They argue that any person who helps another individual to die is guilty of the most serious crime—murder.

Different types of euthanasia

Euthanasia is often categorized into three main types: voluntary, non-voluntary and involuntary.

Voluntary euthanasia usually involves incurably ill patients who are determined to die in order to end their suffering. They are able to explain their wishes to their doctors and their families. The course of action that follows is described either as "active" or "passive." Active euthanasia is when the patient takes a fatal dose of a drug. If he or she is unable to do this (due to an inability to swallow, for example), the patient may ask a doctor to administer it. Passive euthanasia involves a doctor withholding the treatment necessary for life to continue, for example, switching off a life support system or choosing not to give certain drugs.

Non-voluntary euthanasia occurs when someone other than the patient has to make the decision about whether he or she should die. This is usually because the patient is unable to make a decision, or to make his or her wishes known: for example, a terminally ill baby, or a person in a persistent vegetative state (see page 16).

Involuntary euthanasia is when a person wants to live, but his or her life is taken anyway. This is usually deemed to be murder.

Laws and guidelines

Supporters of euthanasia argue that detailed laws and guidelines will prevent abuse. They say that humans have the means, and therefore the responsibility, to make death as "good" an experience as possible. Opponents say humans are easily corrupted. They insist that support for euthanasia implies that some lives (for example, those of the disabled or ill) are worth less than others. For many people, this is morally unacceptable.

A good death...

"Just as I believe that good schools should be accessible to all, so I think a good death should be accessible to all. I cannot see one rational reason for not allowing it."

Chris Woodhead, former chief inspector of schools in England, who was diagnosed with motor neuron disease in 2006

. . . or not?

"Two dangerous ideas lie just below the surface of awareness... though they are not usually thought proper to be voiced openly: that there are groups of unfortunate people whom society could well do without, and that they cost a lot of money that could be better spent."

Dr. Brian Pollard, International Association for Hospice and Palliative Care Web site, 2012

Many people say legalizing euthanasia is dangerous. They argue that frail, older people could be persuaded to end their lives for the wrong reasons, for example, to save money or to avoid becoming a burden to their families.

A noble end?

Euthanasia has a long history. It was used in ancient Greek and Roman society to avoid public disgrace or military defeat. In classical Athens, city magistrates kept a supply of poison to be issued at their discretion. Euthanasia was supported by the philosophers Plato and Socrates, but opposed by the physician Hippocrates, who wrote: "I will give no deadly medicine to any one if asked, nor suggest any such counsel."

Changing attitudes

With the spread of Christianity, opposition to euthanasia grew. Early Christian teachers such as Thomas Aquinas said that both suicide and assisted dying were wrong because they harmed the person in question, as well as others who had a connection to the person. Most importantly, they said death should be in God's hands. The view that human life was sacred held sway for hundreds of years, despite the fact that human behavior often contradicted this belief. For example, impoverished families in the Middle Ages regularly practiced infanticide, a kind of involuntary euthanasia, as birth control. Suffocation was usually the favored method.

The euthanasia movement

The rise of a formal movement in support of euthanasia began in the 1800s. Midway through the century, drugs such as morphine and chloroform began to be used to "treat the pains of death." Then, in 1870, debate about the issue of euthanasia was sparked off by a speech given at the Birmingham Speculative Club (in Birmingham, UK) by a teacher called Samuel Williams. Members of this small club met regularly to discuss the issues of the day. In his speech, Williams proposed the use of anesthetics (numbing drugs) and morphine to end the life of a terminally ill patient. The speech was published, and his views were supported by several leading physicians.

In 1894, in the United States, the political leader and abolitionist Robert Ingersoll argued that if a person were suffering from a terminal illness, he or she should be allowed to take his or her own life. In 1906, the politician Henry Hunt attempted to legalize euthanasia by introducing a bill into the General Assembly of Ohio, but it failed to pass.

The argument about the right of humans to choose their own destiny versus God as the ultimate decision-maker still underpins much of the thinking about euthanasia today.

Royal euthanasia

In the UK, the royal physician gave the dying King George V a fatal dose of morphine and cocaine in 1936. According to the physician's notes, this was done to ensure a pain-free end—and to hasten the king's death for announcement in the morning papers. This "mercy killing" coincided with proposed legislation in Parliament to legalize euthanasia, which was unsuccessful.

A statue in London commemorates the British monarch George V. The details of the king's "mercy killing" were kept secret for 50 years.

An End to Suffering?

When it comes to end-of-life decisions, how much power should rest in the hands of the medical profession? Given that a doctor's primary role is to preserve life, can it ever be acceptable for a physician to help a patient to die?

Most of us would accept that doctors are the people best qualified to judge a patient's state of health and chances of recovery.

Does it therefore follow that we should look to doctors to advise when assisted dying would be appropriate?

Difficult decisions

Doctors are taught to place patient welfare at the top of their list of priorities; their training forbids them to consider the termination of a patient's life. In reality, however, doctors are already required to make such judgments about a patient's care. They must weigh up the side-effects of treatment against the length of life remaining for a patient, and the possible impact on the care of others. For example, should a patient in the advanced stages of terminal cancer be resuscitated (brought back to life) in the event of a heart attack? When funds are limited or scarce, should expensive treatment be made available to a person suffering from a fatal condition when it could be used to save the life of another, healthier person?

Supporters of euthanasia argue that, provided the patient requests it, a swift and relatively painless death is preferable to a drawn-out, agonizing one. This will also ensure that resources are directed towards those patients who are likely to benefit the most. Opponents say that the principles of medical ethics (see panel) require doctors to avoid harming a patient (non-maleficence) and to aim to do good (beneficence). They argue that considering anything other than the preservation of life is a serious breach of doctor–patient trust.

(Opposite) **Opponents of euthanasia say legalizing it would give doctors too much power. But supporters say that doctors already make life-and-death decisions when they make choices about patient treatment.**

The four principles

The following four principles form the basis of medical ethics:

- beneficence – the doctor must be well-intentioned towards the patient and aim to do good

- non-maleficence – the doctor must avoid harming the patient

- autonomy – the doctor must treat the patient as a rational person capable of making choices for him or herself

- justice – the doctor must distribute resources, including time and skill, fairly between patients

The practice of medicine

While many argue that "letting" a person die (by withdrawing treatment, for example) is different from actively taking a person's life, others say that, as the end result is the same (death), there is no difference between them. Depending on how you look at

An intravenous (IV) drip in a patient's hand delivers pain relief (or other fluids) directly into the bloodstream. High doses of painkillers may be needed to manage severe pain in a terminally ill patient.

Duty of care

"A doctor's commitment to acting for patients' good creates a clear obligation to help a patient avoid an agonizing, protracted death. Allowing a patient to suffer when the suffering could be ended is an obvious violation of the duty of beneficence."

Professor Rosamond Rhodes, Mount Sinai School of Medicine, New York, US, 1998

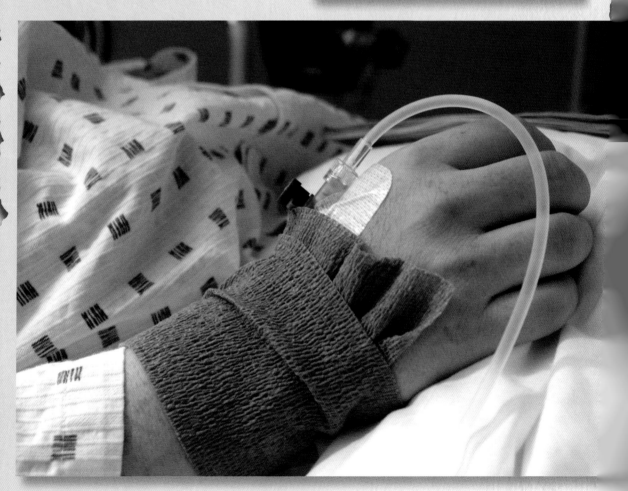

it, switching off a life-support machine can either be interpreted as withdrawing treatment (passive euthanasia), or as a deliberate action that results in the ending of a patient's life (active euthanasia).

The doctrine of double effect

Doctors often use painkillers to treat terminally ill patients, the effects of which may also hasten death. For example, high doses of morphine may be used to relieve acute pain and hopefully improve the patient's comfort, even though doctors know that such doses make it likely the patient will die sooner. This is known as the doctrine of double effect. Wouldn't it be preferable to make euthanasia legal so that doctors could be more open about the methods they use? For supporters of euthanasia, the answer is yes. Hastening death is sometimes in a person's best interests—people should be allowed to die with dignity and not forced to suffer.

Opponents say that euthanasia is never in a person's best interests. Hastening death is unacceptable and undermines doctors' and nurses' commitment to saving lives. It also fails to take into

Subject to abuse

"Those who will be most vulnerable to abuse, error, or indifference are the poor, minorities, and those who are least educated and least empowered. This risk does not reflect a judgment that physicians are more prejudiced or influenced by race and class than the rest of society—only that they are not exempt from the prejudices manifest [that exist] in other areas of our collective life."

From "When Death Is Sought," 1994, report by the New York State Task Force on Life and the Law

account the possible margin of error. What if the diagnosis is wrong and the patient is not terminally ill? What if a patient's demand for euthanasia is actually a cry for help? What if new treatments are developed that could be offered to the patient? Ultimately, opponents claim, legalizing euthanasia would endanger the lives of patients while protecting doctors from prosecution.

Life support

In August 1989, the parents of Anthony Bland, a 19-year-old man in a persistent vegetative state (PVS), asked for their son to be allowed to die. Earlier that year, Bland had been severely injured when he was one of many hundreds of people crushed against security fences at the Hillsborough football stadium in Sheffield, UK. Now, months later, while "alive" in the sense that he could breathe and digest unaided, Bland could not see, hear, communicate or feed himself. His parents believed he would not want to continue living in this condition. The hospital doctors asked the High Court of England and Wales to allow them to let Bland die by withdrawing his feeding tubes; in 1993, permission was granted. Bland became the first patient in British legal history to die through the withdrawal of food and fluid with the deliberate intention of bringing about death.

Was this action morally right? Supporters of non-voluntary euthanasia believe it is wrong to keep people alive artificially (unable to survive without intervention) and make them undergo treatment they might not want. They ask, if there is no quality of life, what is the point in living? Keeping a patient on life support is expensive—the money could be better spent helping patients who have a real chance of recovery. Supporters also argue that, had euthanasia been legal, Bland could have been helped to die more quickly; instead, he suffered the slower death of starvation and dehydration.

Life and death decision

Opponents of non-voluntary euthanasia believe it is wrong to withdraw life support because there is always a chance, however slight, that the patient might recover. If the patient has no means of expression, what gives anyone else the right to decide whether he or she lives or dies? Opponents say

His spirit has left him. . .

"…to his parents and family [Tony Bland] is dead. His spirit has left him and all that remains is the shell of his body."

Sir Stephen Brown, President of the Family Division of the High Court, 1993

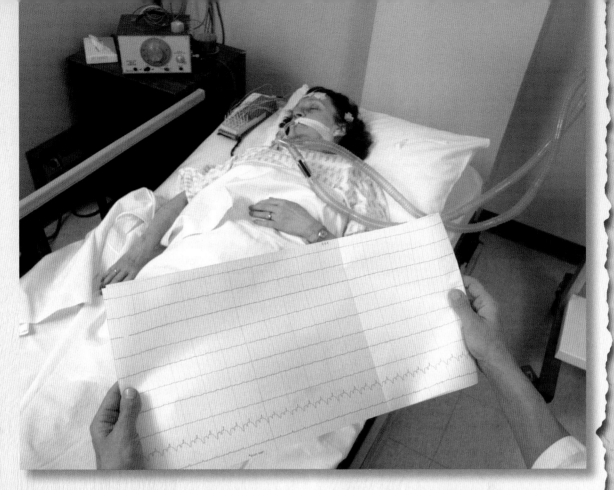

A nurse looks at an electroencephalogram (EEG) at the bedside of a patient on life support. EEG tests measure and record the electrical activity of the brain in PVS patients.

life support machines should not be switched off for reasons of cost. Recent developments in imaging techniques have discovered reactions in the brains of PVS patients—does this mean we need to re-assess our understanding of what the condition means? Opponents argue that PVS patients still retain their humanity, so how can euthanasia be justified? However, if the patient is able to communicate a desire to die, should this wish be honored?

Some measure of improvement?

"Statistics indicate that, when a diagnosis of PVS has been made, that diagnosis may be wrong or, alternatively, even if it is correct, the possibility of some recovery, of some measure of improvement, cannot be excluded."

Gerard Right QC, Catholic Medical Quarterly Web site, 1999

Mental anguish

While euthanasia is most often discussed in relation to terminally ill patients, it is also an issue that relates to people suffering from mental illness. The central question is should doctors allow patients suffering from mental anguish, which causes unbearable suffering, to choose euthanasia? Many people would argue that a person suffering from a mental illness such as depression is unlikely to be able to make rational decisions. The symptoms of many mental illnesses are treatable with the right kind of medication. A severely depressed person might choose to die but equally, given the relevant treatment, may opt to live.

In 2007, the high court in Switzerland ruled that people with serious mental illness could be helped by doctors to take their own lives. A similar law has existed in the Netherlands since 2002 (see page 31). In fact, most psychiatrists and doctors are extremely unwilling to help a mentally ill patient to die because of the many difficult moral and ethical questions this issue raises.

Curable, or not?

Because it is "invisible," mental illness is often perceived differently from physical illnesses such as cancer. Yet the suffering caused by permanent, incurable mental disorders can make life unbearable for a patient. Psychiatrists have to judge whether a person's mental state is curable or not. Meanwhile, some desperate patients who are unable to get professional help to end their lives may try to kill themselves anyway. Sometimes a patient may ask for euthanasia at a time when he or she is not depressed because the thought of their mental anguish returning is too much to bear. Then the psychiatrist has an almost

Death wish

" A distinction has to be made between a death wish which is an expression of a curable, psychiatric disorder and which requires treatment, and [a death wish] which is based on a person of sound judgment's own well-considered and permanent decision, which must be respected."

From the 2007 ruling by the Swiss High Court

impossible decision to make. Should the psychiatrist persist in helping the patient find a new perspective on life, however hopeless it may seem?

Finding the right professional help is vital for people experiencing mental health problems, particularly those having suicidal thoughts.

Not of sound mind

"Never kill yourself when you are suicidal—you are not yourself then."

In "Why safe euthanasia Is a myth," a psychiatrist argues that people with mental illness should never be offered euthanasia because their condition makes their decision liable to change and therefore unsafe

Euthanasia and old age

In 2011, 84-year-old Nan Maitland, a right-to-die campaigner, chose physician-assisted suicide in Switzerland in preference to continuing on into old age. She suffered from arthritis, but was not terminally ill. The former doctor who assisted her had already been struck off the medical register for helping a patient to kill himself six years earlier. Pro-euthanasia campaigners would

More pain than pleasure

"For some time, my life has consisted of more pain than pleasure and over the next months and years the pain will be more and the pleasure less. I have a great feeling of relief that I will have no further need to struggle through each day in dread of what further horrors may lie in wait."

Right-to-die campaigner Nan Maitland, 2011

The real agenda

"This case, involving an elderly woman with arthritis who was actively assisted by fellow campaigners to kill herself, yet again exposes the real agenda of the pro-euthanasia lobby. The true aim of those campaigning for a change in the law... is to allow anyone who requests it, regardless of their age or health, to be helped to end their lives."

Dr. Peter Saunders of the anti-euthanasia group Care Not Killing

argue that Nan Maitland's choice was made freely, and the act of carrying it through was respectful of her human rights. Opponents would say that the doctor actively influenced her to make the choice, and the existence of legalized euthanasia in Switzerland allowed him to act according to his own personal agenda.

Financial concerns

Opponents argue that any law in favor of euthanasia could make it easier for

(Opposite) **Pro-euthanasia campaigners say that people have a right to choose if they wish to die. Opponents argue that vulnerable people can be pressured to make a decision that may not be in their best interests.**

vulnerable people to be persuaded into assisted dying. Elderly people, or people with disabilities, may fear that they are becoming a financial burden on their families. Is this a good enough reason to request euthanasia? Opponents of euthanasia argue that it is not, and that the solution lies in good-quality care for the elderly and those who cannot manage on their own. But such care is expensive, and, with increasingly long-lived populations, it is often in short supply.

The cost of euthanasia drugs to end a life is typically around US$35 to $45; the cost of long-term care could be a thousand times more. In general, health-care providers are under pressure to cut costs, and many people fear that any law in favor of euthanasia could be used as a means of containing costs by such companies. In the United States, many thousands of people are not covered by medical insurance and therefore do not have access to quality health-care services. Opponents fear that euthanasia could potentially be a form of oppression against those who are uninsured—typically the working poor, minorities and the unemployed. In such circumstances, what pressure might be put on older, seriously ill or disabled patients to choose to die?

The Role of Relatives

How far should relatives be involved in a patient's life and death choices? Does allowing a person to die mean that their loved ones are spared unnecessary suffering? Or is there a danger of family members abusing their role?

Protection from family

"...the terminally ill are a class of persons who need protection from family, social, and economic pressures, and who are often particularly vulnerable to such pressures because of chronic pain, depression, and the effects of medication."

From the State of Alaska's arguments that assisted suicide is dangerous (Sampson et al. v. State of Alaska, *2001*)

In 2004, Baroness Mary Warnock, a medical ethics expert, announced she would consider euthanasia if she became a nuisance to her family in old age. Warnock said she would be reluctant to move into a nursing home because they are "a

Baroness Warnock sits on the House of Lords Select Committee on Euthanasia in the UK. She is an outspoken supporter of assisted suicide. She argues that if a person finds life intolerable, then a quick, painless death is the humane solution.

A time of my choosing

"My father, who was suffering from cancer and no longer wished to live, died as he chose: in peace and dignity, with my mother beside him. I passionately hope that, if I too were terminally ill, and was finding life unbearable, I could be allowed to die at a time of my choosing."

Rosemary Brown OBE,
Dignity in Dying patron

terrible waste of money."
Her words prompted an angry response from charities working with older people, who argued that, rather than advocating euthanasia, the system of support should be improved.

Family decision?

The increasing number of people surviving into old age begs the question of how most families will be able to manage the amount of care that will be necessary in the future. Should this factor influence a person's choice when it comes to ending his or her own life? Opponents of euthanasia argue that involving family members in such a decision is unacceptable because the burden of responsibility and guilt is too great. They say there is always a danger that someone might persuade an elderly relative to end his or her life for the wrong reasons—to inherit money, for example.

After death

Some supporters of euthanasia believe that people have the right to involve relatives in their decisions. They emphasize the fact that voluntary euthanasia should only be available to terminally ill, mentally competent adults, and within strict legal safeguards. But what happens to relatives after the death of the affected person? In 2002 Diane Pretty, a terminally ill British woman, fought a legal battle to allow her husband, Brian, to help her die. She wanted a commitment that he would not be prosecuted after her death. She lost her case, and died soon after as a result of breathing difficulties caused by motor neuron disease. Brian Pretty said that, as a result of the court's decision, his wife had been forced to go through the one thing she most feared—choking and suffocation as a result of her condition.

Safeguards and living wills

Euthanasia is legal in the US state of Oregon. There are, however, numerous safeguards in place. The law requires that two independent doctors carry out tests on the patient to ensure he or she is capable of making the decision mentally. The patient must then make two spoken requests and one written request for assistance in dying, to be checked by two independent witnesses. Family members are not allowed to be witnesses. People who are not mentally competent, for example patients with dementia or Alzheimer's, are not eligible for medical help to die.

Supporters of euthanasia argue that such safeguards provide sufficient protection for the patient. They also remove the responsibility of taking difficult decisions from family and friends. But opponents say that even if legal safeguards exist, they will not stop some people being persuaded to choose euthanasia when they do not really want it.

Living wills

In 1967, Luis Kutner, an American lawyer and human rights activist, suggested the first living will. But it was the Karen Ann Quinlan case that brought the argument about living wills to the fore. In 1975, at the age of 21, Quinlan was left in a persistent vegetative state after swallowing alcohol and drugs at a party. With no hope that she would ever recover consciousness, her parents fought through the US courts for her right to come off the machine that was keeping her alive. In 1976 the New Jersey Supreme Court ruled in their favor. Although Quinlan was taken off life support, she continued to live for another nine years in a coma before eventually dying of pneumonia. The issues raised by the Quinlan case resulted in legislation to allow the creation of living wills, sometimes also called advanced directives.

Planning ahead

In the case of a seriously ill patient who cannot communicate, it can help relatives and doctors if this person has previously made a living will. For example, patients with degenerative illnesses can draw up

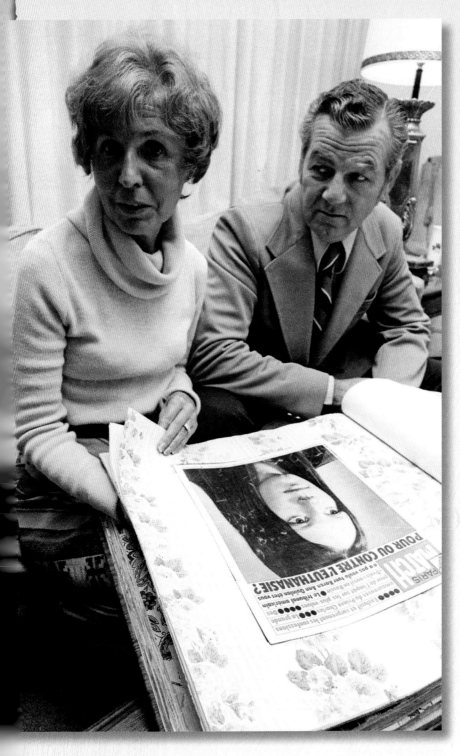

Joseph and Julia Quinlan with a scrapbook dedicated to their daughter, Karen Ann. They fought a legal battle to allow their daughter to die.

also instruct that doctors continue to treat the patient, regardless of suffering. In 2007, it was estimated that 41 percent of US citizens had completed a living will. In 2009, Barack Obama became the first US president to announce publicly that he had one.

Supporters say that living wills allow patients to have control over their own treatment. Opponents argue that it's difficult for a healthy person to anticipate how he or she will feel when the time comes

documents when they are still able to specify exactly what they want to happen to them. Living wills may give instructions to block treatment and induce death, but they may

to enact the living will. It's possible that some patients may change their minds about their living wills, but be unable to communicate this to those around them.

The Role of Religion

For many people, religion is central to their lives. For others, religion may only be significant in relation to rites of passage such as birth, marriage and death. However people experience it, there is no doubt that religion can provide understanding and comfort for those facing death. It is therefore unsurprising that it plays a central role in law and ethical matters; as far as religion is concerned, euthanasia is a controversial subject.

A higher power

People of most religions oppose euthanasia on moral grounds; they state that only a higher power can decide when to end life. Most Christians do not approve of euthanasia, and some absolutely forbid it. The Roman Catholic Church does not accept that people have a right to die, and believes that euthanasia (and suicide) are a rejection of God's absolute authority over life and death. Similarly, followers of Judaism and Islam do not agree with euthanasia because they regard all human life as sacred.

According to these arguments, no human being has the moral authority to assist a patient to die. Many Christians maintain that it is wrong to interfere with the process of dying, even if there is extreme pain, because this is often a time of great spiritual intensity. Some believers point to Jesus's suffering on the cross as proof that there is a spiritual value to suffering.

An act of murder

"Any positive act designed to hasten the death of the patient is equated with murder in Jewish law, even if the death is hastened only by a matter of moments. No matter how laudable [praiseworthy] the intentions of the person performing an act of mercy-killing may be, his deed constitutes an act of homicide [murder]."

Rabbi J. D. Bleich, 2005

Continuous cycle

Members of some Eastern religions take a rather different view. Hindus and Buddhists see life as part of a continuous cycle of birth, death and rebirth. There are two Hindu views on euthanasia: that it interferes with this cycle and is therefore a bad thing to do; or that by helping to end a painful life, a person is doing good. Buddhist thinking suggests that suicide (and therefore euthanasia) is only acceptable for the very few people who have achieved enlightenment (a state of deep spiritual insight).

Pope Benedict XVI (center) strongly defends the view of the Roman Catholic Church that euthanasia is morally wrong. He has said that "euthanasia is a false solution to the drama of suffering" and that, for the Catholic Church, "the deliberate decision to deprive an innocent human being of his life is always morally evil."

Lord of death

"'Death,' we are told, 'should be left to God.' We do not leave birth to God. We space births. We prevent births. We arrange births. Man should learn to become the lord of death as well as the master of birth."

Leslie Weatherhead, Methodist minister, The Christian Agnostic, *1965*

27

Do not kill?

Many supporters of euthanasia argue that one reason why it is illegal in most countries is because religious groups continually lobby (campaign) against pro-euthanasia legislation. Supporters say history proves that people can easily be persuaded to kill others in the name of religion, in contradiction to the Christian commandment often used by anti-euthanasia campaigners: "Thou shalt not kill."

A minority of Christians believe that God has given humans the intelligence to take charge of their destiny and we have a moral duty to exercise that power. Jesus said, "Do unto others as you would have them do unto you." By this token, if you were suffering, might you not want someone to help you end your life?

An eye for an eye?

Some religious people oppose any form of euthanasia, yet support the death penalty for crimes such as murder. They argue that a person who takes life must forfeit his or her own right to life as punishment. Is this a logical argument?

The Schiavo case

In 2005, Michael Schiavo won the right to allow doctors to remove the

Natural means of preserving life

"I should like particularly to underline how the administration of water and food, even when provided by artificial means, always represents a natural means of preserving life, not a medical act."

Pope John Paul II, speaking about the Terri Schiavo case in 2004

feeding tube from his wife, Terri, so that she could be allowed, as he put it, to "die with dignity." Terri had been in a persistent vegetative state after collapsing 15 years previously, and doctors said she would never recover. Terri's parents fought Michael, her legal guardian, for seven years through the courts in an effort to keep their daughter alive. They were supported by the then US president, George W. Bush, who tried unsuccessfully to overturn the decision of the court in Florida to remove the feeding tube. Eventually Michael won his fight and Terri died in his arms.

The Schiavo case had a strong religious context. Both of Terri's parents are Roman Catholics, and their daughter was a devout Catholic too. Her parents firmly believed that Terri would never have consented to any form of assisted suicide. They were supported by a wide-ranging alliance of high-ranking officials from the Roman Catholic Church, including the Pope, and many evangelical Protestant Christians in the United States. President Bush, a born-again Christian, described his involvement in the Schiavo case as an attempt to preserve "a culture of life." But others described it as "a crass display of pandering to the Christian right" from a man who, as governor of Texas, had approved the execution of 152 prisoners.

Condemned

"I was condemned by the President, the majority leaders of the House and Senate, the governor of Florida, the Pope, and the right-wing media, all because I was doing what Terri—the woman I loved— wanted…"

Michael Schiavo, 2006

Protesters outside the hospice where Terry Schiavo (shown on the placard with her mother) lay dying in 2005. While most of the protests were non-violent, Michael Schiavo received numerous death threats for making the decision to let his wife die.

Euthanasia and the Law

Voluntary euthanasia is illegal in all but a few countries in the world. In a democracy, laws exist for the good of the many. But in some cases, compassion for another person's suffering may lead an individual to carry out a "mercy killing" and risk paying the penalty of the law. So should any form of euthanasia be legal?

Punishment

Should a person who helps someone else to die be punished, even if it is clear that he or she was acting out of compassion and in accordance with the person's wishes? If so, what form should the punishment take? In the UK, assisting suicide carries a jail term of up to 14 years. Yet several terminally ill people have challenged this law, in order to allow family members

Portland, Oregon, 2006: terminally-ill cancer patients Lovelle Svarte *(left)* and Charlene Andrews *(center)* react with delight at news of a US Supreme Court ruling that upheld the physician-assisted suicide law in the state.

to help them to die at some future point without the threat of punishment (see page 23). Is imprisonment really an appropriate response to this "crime"?

The Dutch experience

Voluntary euthanasia has been legal in the Netherlands since 2002. The largest number of cases involve cancer patients, and most people choose to die at home. Supporters say that most Dutch people feel there are sufficient safeguards for patients. Euthanasia remains a criminal offense if the doctor involved does not follow a set of very specific rules. The patient must be conscious and experiencing "unbearable pain." He or she must request euthanasia voluntarily and repeatedly, and must be given time and opportunity to consider the alternatives. A second, independent doctor must also be consulted.

Opponents express concern that although the practice may have started with terminally ill cancer patients, it has since broadened to other groups, including psychiatric patients, sick children and cases of mental illness. In 2012, the launch of a "mobile euthanasia unit" caused an outcry in the Netherlands. The unit is designed to help people whose own

Laws around the world

- voluntary (active) euthanasia is legal in the Netherlands, Belgium and Luxembourg

- assisted suicide (where the patient takes an active role in the drug administration) is legal in Switzerland and in the US states of Washington, Oregon and Montana

- passive euthanasia is legal in Ireland, Mexico and Colombia

- in Albania, if three or more family members consent, passive euthanasia can be applied

- in 2011 the Indian government legalized passive euthanasia after it decided that doctors could withdraw life support from a woman who had been in a persistent vegetative state for 37 years

doctors refuse to assist them with euthanasia. Despite being governed by the Netherlands' strict laws, many people fear that initiatives such as this could extend euthanasia to people who are simply "weary of life" rather than terminally ill.

"Suicide tourism"

The illegality of euthanasia does not imply a duty to preserve life at all costs. As we have seen, it is lawful for doctors to give pain relief that risks death, as long as death is not what is intended (the doctrine of double effect; see page 15). However, if a person lives in a country where euthanasia is illegal, and he or she wants support to end his or her life, that person will need to make the journey to a country in which active euthanasia is legal. This means it is only an option for those people well enough to travel and with enough money to fund the trip. Some individuals may die sooner than they really want to, for fear of becoming too ill to travel if they leave it too late.

Dignitas

Over the past decade, more than 1,000 people, most of them terminally ill, have gone to the Dignitas clinic in Zurich, Switzerland, to end their lives. They have traveled long distances and paid a lot of money to achieve this end. Critics call the practice "suicide tourism" and say that Dignitas is a money-making operation that actively promotes

a "culture of death." They accuse it of secrecy (Dignitas has repeatedly refused to open its finances to the public). They say the Swiss government's decision to allow foreigners to come to Switzerland for assisted suicide makes a mockery of the law in the patient's country of origin and sends the wrong message to terminally ill people.

Supporters argue that organizations such as Dignitas provide a service for people who otherwise would try to take their lives at home and, as a consequence, might suffer much more. They insist that the safeguards imposed by Dignitas

Lack of assessment

"People traveling to Dignitas don't seem to be properly assessed so many patients are not terminally ill, some are psychologically unwell— they are not the sort of people we feel should have assisted suicide."

Dr. John Wiles of the anti-euthanasia alliance Care Not Killing

are very strict. However, many people think it is outrageous for people who want to die with dignity to be forced to travel to a foreign country to do so.

A house, near Zurich in Switzerland, where Dignitas helps people to die. Dignitas says that giving help and support to suffering people who want to die demonstrates the utmost respect for human life.

Traveling to die

"I feel embarrassed that people from this country [the UK] have to go, cap in hand, to die in Switzerland."

Terry Pratchett, author, who was diagnosed with Alzheimer's disease in 2008

The "Slippery Slope"

Some people fear that any change in the laws against euthanasia could open the door to unintended consequences in the future. This is known as the "slippery slope" argument. Those who support this view ask: if voluntary euthanasia were to become legal, how long would it be before people who might not necessarily choose euthanasia would be pushed towards it?

Many opponents of euthanasia fear that any moves towards legalization could blur the distinction between right and wrong. They believe that the supreme value attached to the sanctity of human life would be undermined. They also think that any acceptance of euthanasia implies that some lives—for example, those of poor, old and disabled people—are less valuable than others. They say that the pressure on doctors, hospitals, insurers and governments to save money, together with the limited availability of palliative care, means the most vulnerable members of society would inevitably be targeted.

Strict conditions

Most supporters of euthanasia do not believe the slippery slope is a serious argument. They argue that it is quite possible to make a law that states that voluntary euthanasia or physician-assisted suicide should be performed only under certain conditions. They believe it is possible to police this law against, for example, undue

No limit?

"…even if the…narrow category of terminal illness is chosen at the outset… the logic of suicide as a compassionate choice for patients who are in pain or suffering suggests no such limit."

From "When Death Is Sought," 1994, report by the New York State Task Force on Life and the Law

Disabled protesters from the action group Not Dead Yet gather in October 2005 outside the US Supreme Court, in Washington, D.C., to protest against physician-assisted suicide.

pressure from families. Supporters argue that a person's right to be free of terrible suffering is morally stronger than another person's claim to be protected against unwanted pressure to choose to die. They say the slippery slope argument, that "murder might lurk under the cloak of kindness," stirs up unnecessary general panic.

Offering relief?

"The duty to offer relief to 'grossly suffering terminal' patients... is stronger than the duty to spare patients whose vulnerability might be increased by the granting of that relief."

Nigel Biggar,
Aiming to Kill: The Ethics of Suicide and Euthanasia, *2004*

Palliative care

Hospices are places where terminally ill people can go to be nursed until they die. Hospices offer good palliative care and enable people to die with dignity through the use of modern painkillers. But providing palliative care is hard work, time-consuming and costly. It is certainly easier, cheaper and quicker to end a patient's life with a cocktail of drugs or an injection.

Opponents fear that the introduction of euthanasia will reduce the availability of palliative care, because health-care organizations will want to choose the most cost-effective ways of dealing with dying patients. Hospice teams generally prefer to distance themselves from the idea of euthanasia because they believe it would damage the trust they work so hard to gain with their patients. Hospice carers help patients with an incurable illness to focus on making the most of whatever time they have left. Opponents of euthanasia argue that the legalization of assisted dying would undermine this positive attitude.

Not enough?

Supporters of euthanasia say that while palliative care is important,

Better pain control

"...these pain-specialist [hospice] physicians see the solution to the public debate [about euthanasia] in improved methods of pain control, symptom control, and increased resources for pain research... Better pain control means less call for assisted suicide, they say."

Margaret Pabst Battin,
Ending Life: Ethics and
the Way We Die, 2005

occasionally it is not enough. Some doctors estimate that a small percentage of terminally ill patients do not receive satisfactory pain relief, despite hospice care. There are also people whose belief in free will extends to the freedom to choose the circumstances of their own death. When terminally ill, such people may choose assisted dying in preference to a slow decline characterized by dependency, pain and the loss of alertness, dignity and privacy. Others may be grateful for palliative care up to a point, but beyond that would prefer to die rather than continue living in a helpless and distressed state.

However, some people argue that euthanasia and palliative care are not so firmly opposed as they appear to be, since both share concern for the management and reduction of suffering (physical and mental) at the end of life.

A patient strokes a therapy dog handled by a hospice care worker.

Dignity and choice

"If I truly believe in the principles by which we work in palliative care, which are to respect our patients, to respect their need for respect, for dignity and choice, I need to be prepared to listen to patients who wish to request [assistance to die]."

Dr. Carole Dacombe, medical director of St. Peter's Hospice, Bristol, UK, 2005

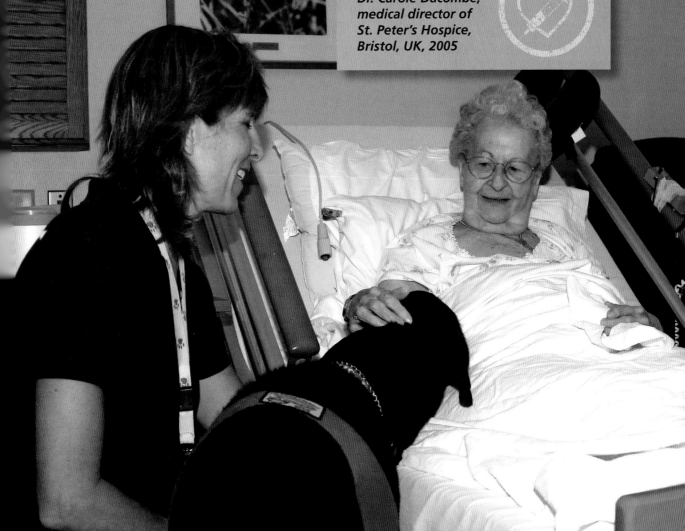

The uncertainty principle

One of the arguments against euthanasia is that once the moral case against the idea of taking life has been lost, it is more difficult to make other moral arguments. Opponents of euthanasia fear that this will ultimately lead to the killing of people whom society regards as less "desirable." They say that if you allow one exception to the law regarding the deliberate taking of life, then other exceptions will be made. Legalization might even allow unbalanced individuals to use euthanasia for their own ends.

A killer's charter?

Supporters of euthanasia say that properly drafted laws would prevent bad practice. They point out that there is a huge difference between killing people who ask for death and killing people without their permission.

In the United States, one of the most controversial figures in the euthanasia debate was Dr. Jack Kevorkian. Known as "Dr. Death," Kevorkian claimed to have helped at least 130 terminally ill people to

Dr. Jack Kevorkian in court in 1996. He was found guilty of second-degree murder and imprisoned in 1999. He was released on parole in 2007, on the condition that he did not help anyone else to die. He himself died in 2011.

The eugenics movement

Adolf Hitler based the Nazi extermination program on his interpretation of the theory of eugenics. This was the belief that the human race could be improved by the scientific control of breeding. Eugenicists declared that many human traits were genetic, and that people who came from genetically "good" families were superior to people who came from genetically "poor" ones. The aim was to improve society by encouraging the "good" families to have more children and the "poor" families to have fewer, or none. Eugenics became very fashionable in the early 1900s, but following the appalling atrocities of the Nazi extermination program, the theory was largely abandoned.

end their lives between 1990 and 1998. His defiance of the law led eventually to his imprisonment in 1999. His supporters saw him as a force for good, who made people think about the issues around physician-assisted suicide. His opponents viewed him as a "reckless instrument of death."

Legal murder?

Opponents argue that the legalization of euthanasia could lead to a nightmare scenario, in which an extremist government uses euthanasia to murder its citizens. Such a government might decide that certain groups of people, the sick or disabled, for example, were a burden on society. It might then introduce

euthanasia as a way of dealing with this "social problem." This occurred in Germany during the 1930s and 1940s, when the Nazi regime carried out the mass murder of "undesirables" such as Jews, homosexuals and disabled people. The Nazi extermination program was often (inaccurately) described as "euthanasia."

Supporters say that legislating for euthanasia is completely different from sanctioning mass-murder. The main point about the Nazi regime was that it did not kill people because it was in their best interests, it killed them because of a misplaced belief that society would benefit. The Nazis practiced eugenics, not euthanasia.

A Time to Die?

In the past century, scientists have conquered illnesses, found methods by which to manage pain and discovered ever-improving ways to prolong life. Changing attitudes to science and religion have been accompanied by a change in attitude to death and dying. Two thousand years ago, the thought of imminent death, and the way in which he might face it, was probably never far from a Roman soldier's mind. Today, most of us push thoughts of death aside, even though we will all experience it eventually.

Doing harm

"In quixotically trying to conquer death doctors all too frequently do no good for their patients' 'ease' but at the same time they do harm instead by prolonging and even magnifying patients' dis-ease."

Jack Kevorkian, **Prescription: Medicide – The Goodness of Planned Death**, *1993*

Does our trust in modern medicine mean that we are no longer able to contemplate the idea of death? Or does it mean that we think of it differently, with an emphasis on individual rights rather than resigned acceptance—the idea that it is something we do rather than something that happens to us?

Pro-euthanasia groups

There are now pro-euthanasia groups in many countries. Members of these groups see euthanasia as supporting personal choice, autonomy and dignity; they work to inform the public and lobby governments on the issue. Supporters of euthanasia include liberal, humanitarian groups such as Dignity in Dying and Exit International, some members of the medical profession and members of the Unitarian and Methodist churches.

Against euthanasia

Many anti-euthanasia campaigners believe the pro-euthanasia movement is simply a re-emergence

Double standard

"Though often described as compassionate, legalized medical killing is really about a deadly double standard for people with severe disabilities, including both conditions that are labelled terminal and those that are not."

Not Dead Yet, a disability group opposed to the legalization of assisted suicide, 2012

The placard at this pro-euthanasia march in Paris, France, reads: "I want to be able to choose my death." This demonstration was held in 2012, and was organized by the Association for the Right to Die with Dignity.

JE VEUX POUVOIR CHOISIR MA MORT!

of the eugenics movement of the early 20th century (see page 39). They say that while the words used by the pro-euthanasia movement are caring, its overall message is dangerous. Opponents to euthanasia are made up of a range of different political and religious types, including disability-rights activists, civil-rights organizers, advocates for the poor, medical-professional organizations, the Roman Catholic and other Christian churches.

On Death and Dying

In 1969, Elisabeth Kübler-Ross wrote the groundbreaking book *On Death and Dying*. It was based on her experience as a doctor, when she witnessed inadequate and often insensitive treatment of terminally ill patients. She believed doctors turned their backs on these patients because they represented medical failure at a time when medicine seemed to have all the answers.

A merciful death

"Dogs do not have many advantages over people, but one of them is extremely important: euthanasia is not forbidden by law in their case; animals have the right to a merciful death."

Milan Kundera, **The Unbearable Lightness of Being,** *2009*

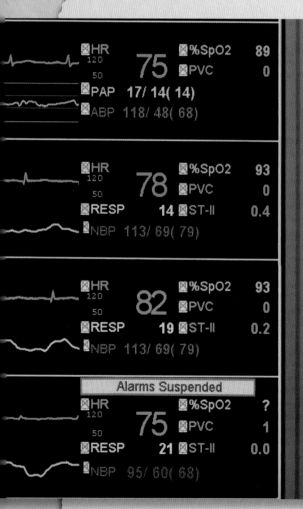

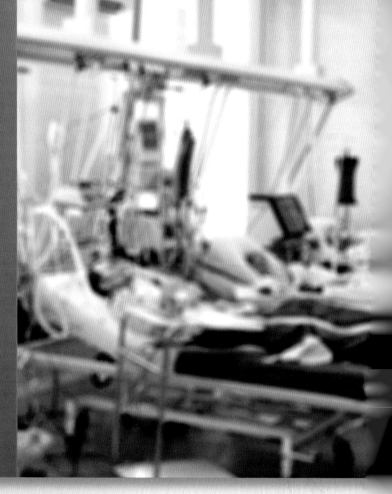

During the following decades, it gradually became more acceptable to talk about dying. This cultural change received legal recognition in 1997, when the US Supreme Court decided that individual states were free to make their own laws regarding physician-assisted suicide (most states opposed it).

Pain control

Opponents of legalized euthanasia insist that pain relief is a preferable option for terminally ill patients. If this fails, they say, there is the option of terminal sedation—inducing a coma that (with the withdrawal of food and liquids) results in death. Supporters argue that accepting terminal sedation is no different from accepting euthanasia, because both are assisted dying in some shape or form.

Self-directed dying

In May 2006 in the UK, the House of Lords blocked a bill that would allow terminally ill people to be helped to die. For the time being, the opponents of euthanasia had triumphed. But supporters continue to insist that legalization will not open the floodgates to non-

(Opposite) **Patients in an intensive care unit. The monitor in the foreground provides doctors with details of the patients' heart rate, blood pressure and so on, all of which helps to assess the amount of pain relief that is required.**

A divine flame

"This life in us... however low it flickers or fiercely burns, is still a divine flame which no man dare presume to put out, be his motives never so humane and enlightened... Either life is always and in all circumstances sacred, or intrinsically [in its nature] of no account; it is inconceivable that it should be in some cases the one, and in some the other."

Malcolm Muggeridge (1903–90), British journalist and editor

voluntary euthanasia. They point to a 1995 investigation of physician-assisted dying in the Netherlands, which found no evidence of a descent down a "slippery slope" towards ignoring people's voluntary choices. Supporters say it is more dangerous to continue without legislation, because this means there is no transparency or monitoring. They hope that, some day, the terminally ill will be able to direct the circumstances of their own death, conscious and alert, before becoming involved in the business of dying itself.

Glossary

abolitionist a person who supported the abolition of slavery

Alzheimer's a brain disease that results in memory loss, confusion and changes in personality and mood

arthritis a condition characterized by pain and swelling in the joints of the body

autonomy literally "self-governing"—the ability of individuals to do or decide something for themselves

beneficence the act of doing good

chloroform a sweet-smelling liquid that was once widely used to numb pain

coma a state of unconsciousness

compassionate caring, sympathetic

degenerative describes an illness in which the affected tissues and organs gradually deteriorate

dementia an incurable disease that causes loss of memory and changing personality

ethical used to describe a practice or belief that fits with accepted principles of right and wrong

eugenics a belief that the human race could be improved by the scientific control of breeding

free will the power to make a choice free from external controls of any kind

infanticide killing a newborn infant

involuntary euthanasia the killing of a person carried out against his or her wishes

living will a document drawn up by a person to specify what treatment they would or would not want in the event of an accident or terminal illness

morphine a drug that gives highly effective pain relief but that is also addictive

motor neuron disease a degenerative disease that causes muscle weakness and wasting

non-voluntary euthanasia the killing of a person who is not capable of expressing his or her wishes; it is conducted on the basis of an estimate of what that person would have wanted

palliative care a branch of health care devoted to the nursing and medical treatment of terminally ill patients

persistent vegetative state (PVS) a medical condition in which patients remain able to breathe and digest unaided, but cannot see, hear, communicate or feed themselves

philosopher a person who investigates existence, knowledge and ethics

physician a medical doctor

prosecute to start legal proceedings against a person or people

psychiatrist a medical doctor who specializes in treating people who are mentally unwell

resuscitated restored to life or consciousness

sedation a state of calm brought about in a patient by the administration of a drug (sedative)

struck off removed from the medical register; no longer licensed to practice medicine

suicide when a person takes his or her own life (if another person helps in this process, it is known as "assisted suicide")

terminal illness a disease or condition that will inevitably result in death

voluntary euthanasia the killing of a person at his or her request, or with his or her consent

For More Information

Books

The Ethics of Euthanasia Craig Donnellan, Independence Educational
    Publishers 2005

Issues Today: Voluntary Euthanasia Lisa Firth, Independence Educational
    Publishers 2012

World Issues: Euthanasia Clive Gifford, Chrysalis 2004

Just the Facts: Euthanasia Linda Jackson, Heinemann Library 2005

Ethical Debates: Euthanasia Kaye Stearman, Wayland 2011

Web Sites

Due to the changing nature of Internet links, Rosen Publishing has
developed an online list of Web sites related to the subject of this
book. This site is updated regularly. Please use this link to access
the list:

http://www.rosenlinks.com/BSOS/Euth

Index